LEOPARD WATCH
(Kiléy Báh)

J.K. Bannavti

Langaa Research & Publishing CIG
Mankon, Bamenda

Publisher:
Langaa RPCIG
Langaa *Research & Publishing Common Initiative Group*
P.O. Box 902 Mankon
Bamenda
North West Region
Cameroon
Langaagrp@gmail.com
www.langaa-rpcig.net

Distributed outside N. America by African Books Collective
orders@africanbookscollective.com
www.africanbookcollective.com

Distributed in N. America by Michigan State University Press
msupress@msu.edu
www.msupress.msu.edu

ISBN: 9956-579-16-5

For Mama Odilia Lantir Fonka Shang who labored to raise me

Note on the Play

Leopard Watch, like its precursor, *Rock of God,* provides us a remarkable window into the underlying rational behind a people's naming culture. This naming culture is what I will briefly attempt to explain.

The Kingdom of Nso is replete with names that closely reference major events, personalities, things and people. One name could refer to the same event or situation but would derive its meaning from the interpretation the person who gave the name attaches to it. The name Bara' (advanced person), may refer to the entry of someone with superior tools into Nso; it may also refer to human-improvement advances introduced by an external culture such as the 'white culture'. Similarly, it could refer to something that negatively impacted a person, family, parent, or people, as a result of the arrival, presence or intervention of this 'advanced person'. Names in Nso, especially those that are not baptismal names,[1] are information markers.

The information basis of Nso names therefore applies to the name Kiléy Báh (Leopard Watch). This is the name of a river (which is now just a rivulet) that runs along the southwestern end of the slope of Tan hill, a semi plateau on the Jakiri–Foumban highway. Kiléy Báh gathers most of its waters from brooks trickling down the spine of Tan.

Part of the history of Kiléy Báh is rooted in the events following the Nso-Bamoun war of 1885. After the success of the Nso over the Bamoun in that war, the Fon of Nso assigned the control and use of Ber (final 'r' is pronounced) and neighboring Ngewir (final 'r' is pronounced) to Shufaay Sov. As a result Shufaay Sov and his people organized "the Fon's periodic hunting expeditions" in which they set the marshy plains on fire and ambushed fleeing animals at one outlet. Shufaay Sov later embarked on a strategy to settle part of his family in Ber and Ngewir in order to start cultivating the land. As soon as the early settlers arrived, hunting and cultivation went on simultaneously. Many members of the Sov family who built their second homes in Ber and Ngewir became expert in regularly setting traps to catch wild animals.

In one of those exercises, Ntumbi of Sov caught a leopard in a trap.[2] This generated a lot of news because of the symbolism[3] that the leopard carries in Nso culture. People thronged to the site to see the beast displayed on a large exposed rock in the river. Through oral transmission of information many people asked others if they have seen the leopard yet; many others returned from the scene with excitement after 'watching' the leopard to narrate the awesome 'spectacle'. Leopard Watch suddenly became synonymous with the river and gradually became the river's name.

And so it is that the play *Leopard Watch* uses a name that is historically based to dramatize the circumstances of a destitute people, a people crippled by fear – fear of a beast that has eluded ambush and desperate hunt; years of major attacks by Manjong, the military force of the Kingdom.

It is interesting, and even ironical that the latest assignment to capture the beast is in the hands of Ngwa', a youth hunting troupe that now doubles as a vigilante force. What this says about Manjong, the direct military force, is left to conjecture; however the fact that the leadership of some of Manjong's vital components is now focused on coaching Ngwa', is a powerful symbol of how nations may need to switch strategies when confronted by predatory forces. Whatever each of us thinks about the youth involvement is left to reason, but it seems the author is underscoring the fact that the fight for collective survival cannot be the responsibility of grown-ups alone. In dire circumstances, even children have to grow up.

As many of us try to understand the foundations of local art in our indigenous cultures, products like *Leopard Watch* help to bring parts of our cultural history to life while attempting to explore legends that would otherwise disappear. JK Bannavti in this play articulates something larger than a simple story of the origin of a river's name. The play seems to question the source of the destruction that our societies are facing. It also seems to suggest that leadership should own up to the damage it has inflicted on society.

Shey Shiyghan Stephen Shemlon, PhD
Somerset, New Jersey, USA

NOTES

---

[1] Baptismal names: This refers to names associated with Nso indigenous religion. Many have referred to them as baptismal names. These names include: Lukong, Tata(h), Ngong, and Tukov (in that descending age order –eldest to youngest- for males) and Biy, Sheh, Ntang, and Kfekfeh, (in that descending age order for females). The first three, for either sex, are applied in association with names of neighboring clans and kingdoms. For instance, a child may be named Lukong Ngoran, in reference to Bangolan, or Biy Wirmvem' in reference to Mvem (Bamoun) kingdom.

[2] Leopard in a trap: In <u>Sov,! Sov! Our Glorious Heritage</u>, (2003) Rev. Fondzefee Charles Tangwa states that: "Amongst the early Sov settlers who made their second homes in Ber and Ngewir were Tata Neneng….Ntumbi, the brother of Tata Neneng is the man that caught the leopard in a trap and placed it by the stream entering Ber. This stream got its name from that act because it was there that people came to view the leopard, kilaybaa" p. 42

[3] Leopard as a symbol: A Leopard /tiger is symbolic of power, resilience and royalty in the Kingdom of Nso. A prince who becomes Fon must be a "leopard-skin prince" meaning one who was conceived on the royal bed. Anecdotal recounts say the rug around the royal bed is a tiger's/leopard's hide.

Dramatis Personae

Fon: King of Bamkov

Tawong: Guardian of the kingdom's sacred shrines and rules

Yewong: Guardian of the kingdom's sacred shrines and rules

Ngarum: Senior prophet and elder of the kingdom

Tamfu: Leader of the male society (Mfu') a strong arm of the entire military organization (Manjong)

Gwei: Herald of Manjong and member of Mfu'. Lantir's husband

Tangwa: Leader of Ngwa', a youth hunting troupe; Befeh's husband

Lantir: Gwei's wife

Befeh: Tangwa's wife

Kibong: Independent business woman: seller of local corn beer

Sunjo: Senior member of Ngwa'

Tantan: Senior member of Ngwa'

Binla: Senior member of Ngwa'

Nwerong: Masquerades serving as security deterrence:

Women: Members of Chong, women's cult.

Men: Manjong singers, drummers and dancers and Ngwa' members

1

ACT ONE

Scene One

(Palace in grass field Cameroon: Fon sits in his throne snoring and drooling intensely. Tawong is by his side. As Yewong walks in, Tawong moves closer to receive her. They start commenting in hushed tones.)

Yewong: Has His Majesty opened his eyes yet?
              Has the chewing stopped?

Tawong: Not yet. The chewing has become worse!
              He chews even in his sleep like a sheep.
              Then suddenly he laps, licks and belches!

Yewong: What could have happened?
              Who turned our King into a dog?

Tawong: Into a beast.
              He chews and yawns;
              Then he groans like a tiger.

Yewong: *(Confidentially)*
              So what will happen now?
              Did he finally agree to something?

Tawong: Yes, we are waiting for Ngarum.

Yewong: That at least is good,
              But is that all?

Tawong: We should know something today!

Yewong: That at least gives me some hope.
             The land cannot be disappearing,
             Disappearing from view and ear,
             While the Fon sleeps!

Tawong: We hope that Ngarum remains Ngarum.[1]
             If he does, we will be sure of a verdict.

Yewong: Else?

Tawong: Else he may punish Ngarum severely.

Yewong: Why would he hurt the only eyes we have
             At a time like this!

Tawong: You never can tell how he will act:
             One moment he is quiet;
             Then the next moment he is a tornado.

Yewong: I hear a male voice approaching.
             Make sure he does not see all this drooling!

Tawong: What can I do about it?
             Better he even sees it.
             That tells him our dire need!

Yewong: Let me go now!
             Chong is visiting the Rock[2] for the yearly
             blessing of the seeds. Yesum suggests we
             should be back before nightfall.

Tawong: You never can be so sure when to come back
             Any time you visit the Rock of God.
             Come to the palace immediately you finish
             from there.

4

Yewong:	I will.

(Exits. A knowingly loud clearing of the throat is heard from the approaching Ngarum. He is visibly startled at the way the Fon is chewing, swallowing, sleeping and drooling. He moves back, and then claps both cupped hands and hum in greetings to the Fon. Fon is a little startled, then goes back to sleep.)

Tawong:	Ngarum! It is always our joy to have you in the palace!

Ngarum:	It is my duty! A palace summons is a palace summons! You always gird your loins for something serious!

Tawong:	*(Pointing to the middle)* Go ahead and put your wares here. *(Realizing that Ngarum is watching the King in utter surprise)* The Lion's mouth makes a waterfall on his chest. *(Pause)* Do not keep shaking your head as if in mourning. *(Examines both King and invitee)* Just get set before we wake up the King.

Ngarum:	I am all set as you can see. A bird about to lay eggs, First readies its nest. *(Spreads a mat in the middle)*

Tawong: (*Claps cupped hands and hums in traditional greeting to the Fon. Fon wakes up with a start, stretches wildly, wipes his face, mouth and nose as if barely dragging himself along.*)

Your Majesty;
The prophet of the land is here.
He is ready for what your Majesty may command.

Fon: (*In sudden rejection and anger*)
Who is that?

Tawong: Ngarum, my King,
The prophet of the land!

Fon: Who brought him here?
Who asked him here?
Did you, Tawong?

Tawong: My Lord must have forgotten
That it was the royal word that
Summoned him

Fon: So it was me?
I asked for him?
How come?

Tawong: Our Majesty alone can tell!

Fon: Well, as long as he does not start trouble!

Tawong: He is a true servant of the kingdom my King;
He would rather kill himself than start trouble

Fon: Let him hurry up!

Tawong: *(To Ngarum)*
             Your Majesty still needs a little more rest
             As you can see for yourself,
             But since your presence is of such importance
             He would want us to start quickly
             So we can also finish quickly

Ngarum: *(In a lot of shock)*
             Who am I to question his Majesty?
             My wares are all on the mat
             And he alone can tell me where to start.

Tawong: So it must be!
             The palace believes your sight is like a sharp
             spear; it never goes out and comes back
             without a rich chunk of meat.
             Now to the questions:
             Why is Bamkov disappearing?
             What beast is eating Bamkov alive?

Ngarum: *(Throws his cowries and looks through them intensely.*
             The Fon watches him very closely and is almost
             panting)
             Your Majesty may like to know this:
             The signs are not very good!
             But let me check this again.
             (Throws his cowries again, scrutinizes them for a
             while, and then shakes his head as if in disbelief. He
             studies them again very closely: He coughs and bows
             his head to the Fon and stares only downward without
             lifting his head. He pronounces)
             The noose, our Majesty is on our neck

Fon: *(Angrily)*
             Is that something new?
             I brought you here to tell me the root of the
             problem.

I did not summon you to tell me that we have a serious problem!
What do you have to tell us?

Ngarum: Why my King should a snake feast on its tail?
It is only committing suicide!
A rat that nests on shrubs in the dry season
Is handing its young to brush fire!
You Majesty,
Only a pig would devour its young out of hunger!

Fon: (*Angrily*)
Now stop that kind of talk!
You fool!
You want to speak to me?
Then clean your mouth!
You speak with food in your mouth:
How would I understand what you have to say?
All I want to know is, where has Bamkov gone wrong?

Ngarum: Royal Majesty,
Our curse is in our hands;
But there is still time, my King.
We can cleanse ourselves and save the kingdom!
(*The Fon gets up and starts pacing in anger, frustration and intimidation*)

Tawong: Are you saying that Bamkov is destroying Bamkov? Are we so full of evil that we are the curse on our head?

Ngarum: I did not say that, my King!

Tawong: If Bamkov is the snake
              Who are the eggs?

Ngarum: My Majesty has mixed it up!

Tawong: You say I have what?
              I have become a stranger to our language?

Ngarum: The palace summoned me,
              But I fear Your Majesty does not want me!

Tawong: Listen to you, Ngarum!
              You have made your choice:
              You have sided against the palace!

Ngarum: I have not said anything to hurt your Majesty;
              Not anything to hurt Bamkov
              Instead, I want to save the land!

Tawong: Oh, you want to save Bamkov!
              From which snake?

Ngarum: (*Losing control of himself*)
              Mighty King, go to the Rock of God.
              The Rock chose Bamkov;
              Bamkov never chose the Rock.
              The decision to survive is ours!

Fon: What?

Ngarum: While the pool is still around,
              The crocodile may feast.
              But it will soon dry up!
              (*The Fon starts to move across to where spears are
              stacked against the wall, as if to pick up one and attack
              his guest, but misses his step, slumps onto the floor and
              starts snoring and drooling. Ngarum seems very shocked*

but Tawong is unshaken).
Oh horror in this land!
Let us get him up Tawong!
(Tawong instead restrains him from touching the Fon)

Tawong: Let your hands not touch him

Ngarum: But the King is on the floor!

Tawong: This is his inner chambers:
            What happens here stays here!

Ngarum: I have never seen anything like this!
            Get Your Majesty up
            To get the Kingdom up.
            He alone can cure the land.

Tawong: My lord, we need you awake.
            He is not finished talking yet.

Fon: *(Half awake)*
            What is he saying?

Tawong: That Bamkov is eating Bamkov!

Fon: *(Wakes up with a start!)*
            What!
            What stupidity!
            He must not throw those his stupid cowries in
            this land.
            He accuses us of our tragedy when we are so
            desperate?
            Send him away before I hack him with an axe.
            I want him out of my Kingdom!
            My Kingdom! My Kingdom!
            Banish him to Kiyung-Ndzen![3]

Prepare the exile wood ash!

Shoot it on his back as he crosses the bridge.
If he resists, do what you have to do!
Call my Akuman[4] to tell me what the idiot has
on his mind
(*Exits Fon: Two Nwerong masquerades appear and
escort Ngarum out. Tawong is in shock*).

(*Enter Tamfu*)

Tawong: Tamfu!
            I am speechless!
            Your Majesty's orders!

Tamfu: What orders?

Tawong: That Ngarum be banished from this land!

Tamfu: What?
            Your Majesty cannot render us blind
            At a time like this!

Tawong;   Oh, are we not blind already!
            I'm afraid we will stay so.
            He now wants to consult his Akuman.

Tamfu: A what? Aku what?
            No! Nwerong has to do something.
            Even you, Tawong, have to do something.

Tawong: What can I do?

Tamfu: Where is Yewong?

Tawong: Headed for the Rock with Chong!

Tamfu:	Any Wintoh?
	One in full term pregnancy
Tawong:	How could you ask that?
	You know it has been a year
	Since His Majesty's illness started;
	No child born on leopard skin[5].
Tamfu:	How then can we stop this?
Tawong:	We are powerless!
Tamfu:	What a Kingdom!
	Ruled by one man:
	One man who is asleep!
	Asleep and angry!
	Angry and hungry!
	Hungry and afraid!
	While we daily bury
	Child and cattle!
	Let us look for Gwei!
Tawong:	And who will look after the King?
	Who will take care of the Palace?
Tamfu:	The palace never goes away
	The King never goes away.
	Come with me! (*Exit: Darkness*)

Scene Two

(Grove with shrubby grass cover; raffia palm in the background and an aged fig tree dominate scene: Two stools stand across from each other. A fresh banana leaf is laid a little away and between the two stools; a number of cowries, short horn, oil calabash and salt are placed on the leaf. Ngarum is not on seat. Two people sounding very much in disagreement and at the top of their voices can be heard approaching. They are holding their spears and machetes ready for possible danger. As they enter, they start calming down)

Gwei: How could he banish Ngarum?

Tamfu: No one knows.
           Ngarum now lives here…
           In a bush!

Gwei: How does he deal with the situation?

Tamfu: His Akuman may have the answer.

Gwei: But I hear the Akuman is only to tell him
           Who of us is against him?

Tamfu: So his war is not against the beast
           But against us?

Gwei: I wish I could be less worried about the land!
           But I am tired of these deaths;
           Tired of the sadness!
           Tired of the silence!
           Tired of the fear!

Tamfu: Oh, stop singing this tired song!
           You have been singing since the break of day.
           Have you become a cricket
           That sings its own dirge?

Gwei: What do you want me to do?
           Where is the King we once had?
           What direction is he facing?

Tamfu: Stop these questions!
           For how long have you been asking them?
           How much has changed?

Gwei: How much has changed?

Tamfu: Yes!
           Has the ground underfoot changed?
           No!
           Have the leaves on the trees changed?
           No!
           Have river Mairin and Mbim[6] changed?
           No!

Gwei: But Bamkov has a King!
           Kings are for when times are hard;
           When the land is in flames!

Tamfu: So what do you want to do now?
           Kill him?
           Our rules of kingship are unique;
           We cannot change our King
           Until he escapes, or disappears,[7]
           Whether times are hard or not;
           Whether we are in flames or not!

Gwei: (*Screaming to the sky in exasperation*)
           Some Mighty hand help Bamkov!
           A land reeling about
           Like a snake without a head

14

Oh haggard Bamkov!
Coiled up like wretched dung!
Your succor is absent.
Oh, blind night traveler
Tossed by the angry storm,
Your palace cannot speak;
The palace cannot wake up
To secure a wretched people!

Tamfu: The palace cannot wake up,
           But we the people have woken up!
           That is why we came here...

Gwei: *(In exasperation)*
           ...To find out the root of the evil in our land!
           We came here to hear what is eating us alive.
           Yet before we left, he summoned his
           Akuman!
           Why could he not just bury a spear into this
           chest!

Tamfu: Sssssh! You are shouting to the grass!
           The grass has ears!

Gwei: Oh let those ears multiply like corn tassels!

Tamfu: And know that even the wind has ears!

Gwei: Let it blow my word into any other ear!

Tamfu: Are you drunk?
           Stop screaming like a mad man!

Gwei: What is wrong in this land?
           Why can I not express my pain the way I feel?
           Because I fear it will reach the palace?

Even the air I breathe has become a threat?
How long shall we continue to fear?
Anything anybody says is right until it gets to
the Fon!
It is always correct until it enters the palace;
Then they paint you hater of Kingdom.
It becomes criminal to raise a question!
They call it insulting the Fon!
It is criminal to wonder;
They call it hurting the throne!
It is criminal to fear;
They call it spreading evil.
It is criminal to dance;
They call it mocking the land!
It is criminal to sing,
If the song is not a dirge!

Tamfu: You may be right
            But let us be very careful

Gwei: (*More and more exasperated*)
            It is criminal to be careful, Tamfu!
            The ground you stand on belongs to the Fon!
            It is criminal to sleep in your bed;
            Manjong will be gathering to drink palm wine
            tomorrow!
            It is criminal to sleep with your wife;
            Chong will be dancing in the market place
            tomorrow!
            It is criminal this!
            It is criminal that!
            Criminals!!!

Tamfu: Well, it is criminal to be here!

Gwei: Criminal to live!

16

Tamfu:	Well, country of criminals then! *(They pause, then listen and look suspectingly around as if something strange were rustling in the bush.)*
Gwei:	Only the grass swaying! *(Tamfu comments hilariously!)*
Tamfu:	Criminal to look!
Gwei:	I know that! *(They laugh as they take their seats)*
Tamfu:	Where is he?
Gwei:	I have not heard even a cough, Not heard footsteps Since we got here!
Tamfu:	How could we hear a thing? You were screaming all over the place. Well, check the calabash. There must be some palm wine left!
Gwei:	Left from last night? I wonder who he was entertaining.
Tamfu:	Could have just been him alone Drowning his pain in palm wine. *(Pause)* The heat and thorny bushes Made the trip here feel like a battle.
Gwei:	I am just happy we never met the leopard. You never know when that beast could pounce.

Tamfu:	He must be scared of two men armed to the teeth.
Gwei:	If the palace sends someone to look for you or me?
Tamfu:	The children will tell them we went to the bush; They will then think we are on a Manjong assignment.
Gwei:	Who; the palace?
Tamfu:	Yes
Gwei:	Not this one!
Tamfu:	What do you mean?
Gwei:	They will start consulting their Akuman all over.
Tamfu:	And the Akuman will tell them everything about where we are?
Gwei:	Oh yes!
Tamfu:	On second thought that is very frightening! *(Thoughtfully)* You know I have a large family and many young grand children!
Gwei:	Stop shivering like a thieving dog, Tamfu!
Tamfu:	But what do you want me to do?

18

Gwei: Be a man!
            There are consequences for everything we do.
            If you are hit doing the right thing
            You welcome the hit.

Tamfu;   A hit is a hit!
            It is painful.

Gwei: Well, he who eats must endure the hunt!
            Good palm wine comes by braving
            mosquitoes.

Tamfu: May be we just have not heard enough from
            that palace.

(Rumbling noise comes across as if from a sudden hurricane: The two men collapse on their stomachs. Thunder and lightning smash through the grove but there is no rain. Rumbling gradually subsides; the men rise in fright.)

            What was that?
            Rain without rain!

Gwei: Strange!
            I have never seen anything like this.

Tamfu: What direction did it come from?
Gwei: From the direction of the Rock.

Tamfu: What does that mean?

Gwei: How would I know?

(As they quiver in their speech, rumbling starts again: They collapse on their stomachs. Thunder and lightning smash through the grove, but there is no rain. Ngarum's voice is heard getting louder; then darkness!)

Ngarum: Bamkov, rise on your feet!
           Clean your seat and ready your feet.
           The Rock is soon throwing a feast:
           A feast that is more than man!
           Ready your legs for the dance.
           Ready for the feast of the elephant!
           The feast of the land is at hand.

           Rise and shake hands with the Rock,
           For He truly looks over your shoulder.
           His messenger is here!
           His messenger is with you!
           Dressed for battle and ready with spears
           Wondering why the curse on the land
           Wondering like the rest of us.

           The Messenger of the Rock is here:
           But knows not about his mission;
           Not even about his armor:
           The armor of the Rock!
           Oh how the Rock can hide us
           Even from ourselves.
           Darkness has swallowed the beast!
           (Ngarum enters his grove and continues to speak)
           See the Messenger shred the beast like a hawk
           a chick!
           The hills are full of beasts fleeing,
           Fleeing at the Messenger's foot steps!
           Oh you eaters of people!
           Beware of the Mighty Builder at His Rock!
           The Rock will split you in anger,
           And your debris will fall like a shower of sand.

           Watch your steps Bamkov!
           The Rock will grow you again like pumpkin
           And tend you like swamp vegetables!

A riddle truly will issue from your ranks
How once upon a time the Rock called you by
name!
(Pauses and senses around.)
I feel the Rock!
It is close here!
I feel it!
Right here!

(He rummages in the dark then starts singing and dancing to a Manjong victory song, but stumbles on a human body. He pulls out his machete and lifts it up to strike when daylight flushes from above. Realizing his stupefied guests, he addresses them in freight as if trying to figure them out, but they are still too overtaken to say anything.)

Tamfu! Tamfu Bamkov!
That must be you.
Whatever you are doing here,
Count yourself very lucky!
You would have been food
For the eagle already. *(Pauses)*
Who is that?
Gwei! Is that face not your own?
Gwei Bamkov!
You lucky sons of the Rock!
I would have made you easy food for the
beast today!

> *(Replacing his machete into the scabbard)*
> Rise up both of you and sit down
> *(He helps them to their feet)*
> You are not in the home of a stranger
> *(Sits down)*
> Although I am not used to visitors in this place.
> What brings our Manjong leaders here?

Tamfu: *(Stare at him silently)*

Gwei: *(Stare at him silently)*

Ngarum: *(Scans them all over and then suddenly gets up and grabs the calabash of palm wine from the neck and shakes for assurance that there is some left inside.)*

> Nothing?
> You suddenly lost your voices?
> You mean you came all the way here for nothing?
> Anyway, take some palm wine.
> That may enliven you a little bit.
> You look like captured warriors
> In the hands of hostile enemies!
> *(Pours them some palm wine and takes his seat)*
> Well…! What brings you here?

Tamfu: The events that have kept the land awake

Ngarum: I am listening!

Tamfu: When the road disappears in the distance
           It is a sign the end of the journey is not in sight!

Ngarum: I know that; I have ears.

Better speak clearly Tamfu!
Stop chewing your words.

Tamfu: But Ngarum, it is like climbing a tree:
              The arms must first grip the stem!

Gwei: (*Very impatient with Tamfu. Furious and breathing
              heavily, bursts out as Ngarum watches him with
              internal admiration and Tamfu in semi shock*)

              Stop spinning around like a whirlwind,
              Tamfu!
              Children are dying
              The land is crying
              Our strength is sagging
              Women are wailing
              Nwerong is shocked
              Manjong is aghast
              The Kingdom is hopeless;
              Yet the Fon is doing nothing!
              Nothing!
              Nothing!

Tamfu: Nothing?

Gwei: He is only drooling
              He sleeps, chews, laps, and swallows!
              Is that stopping Bamkov from annihilation?

Tamfu: I was not playing the chameleon
              Excusing the palace from our pain!
              The palace summoned the prophet
              To find out the cause of the calamity:
              That at least was something!

Gwei: Oh you call that something!

He summoned him to sack him!
Ngarum, is banished,
Banished from eye and ear
Now, our Kingdom is ruled by an Akuman
Turning the Fon against the people
And brother against brother!
And worse than we could think,
Nwerong has refused to talk![8]

Tamfu: But Nwerong is in the palace;
          How would you expect it to talk!

Gwei: Then tell Ngarum so,
          And stop wrapping your words
          Like balls of fufu!
          (Pause)
          Ngarum, worthy servant of the Rock!
          We are here because we seek the truth!
          We seek a direction to make our next step.
          People of the Rock, people of Bamkov,
          Have lost their foothold:
          Word says you were banished for knowing
          too much!
          Ngarum, we want to hear the too much;
          That may unlock the secret of the beast
          And release him to a land
          That no longer knows itself!

Ngarum: *(Knowingly authoritative)*
          Enough!
          I say enough, Gwei!
          Calm your nerves with some palm wine!
          (Serves them)
          Should I be angry because I was chased out?
          I am happy I left because it was not long

24

Before I saw that mother fowl was feeding on
its own eggs.
But do not deceive yourself;
Everything is like the sun:
It rises just as it must set!
 (Pauses)
But I have news for Bamkov!
The long journey is finally over!
The Rock has pronounced!
You two get up and leave!

Gwei: What?

Tamfu: Is that the pronouncement of the Rock?

Ngarum: Get up and leave!

Gwei: We have not…

Tamfu: You have not…

Ngarum: You have ears but cannot hear?
               You have eyes but cannot see?
               L-e-a-v-e!

Gwei: Now?

Tamfu: Now?

Ngarum: Y-e-s, n-o-w!
               A bat must not be out in the day;
               It will become prey!
               You leave.
               I will see you at the sound of the drum.

               (Exit)

Scene Three

(Break of day: Whistling winds, early morning cockcrows and cackling of fowls suggest the presence of a predator. Distant wailings come across in the wind. An exhausted Gwei leans on a pole in front of his house, spear in hand and scabbard slung over the shoulder. Tamfu announces his presence with a cough and Gwei motions him to a seat. They are visibly restless).

Gwei: I have waited since the first cock crow
          When the early screams echoed through the
          night.

Tamfu: Five children killed this morning, all in their
          sleep.
          The beast simply pounced down the back wall
          of their hut
          And tore them and the caretaker sisters to
          pieces.
          Cattle carcasses were strewn all over the field.

Gwei: What do we make of something like this?

Tamfu: It defeats reason completely!
          Manjong has worn itself out in the fight.

Gwei: Haggard Manjong just returned home
          After another long fruitless hunt.

Tamfu: The beast has defied us;
          It has mocked Bamkov

Gwei: Bamkov of tomorrow is cut down like
          Young banana stems in front of our eyes!
          And it seems like we cannot save the
          situation;
          What kind of Manjong leaders are we?

27

Tamfu:	Horrible!
Gwei:	What is the palace saying about today's bad news?
Tamfu:	Nothing yet! I hear he is still head down, drooling and sleeping.
Gwei:	Sleeping, drooling, chewing and consulting his Akuman
Tamfu:	Having banished the prophet of the land into the wilderness.
Gwei:	I am afraid the Fon may not be as lost as we think
Tamfu:	What do you mean?
Gwei:	Even the worst King would have been up Trying one thing or the other No, he must be aware of what some truth we do not know! He fired those who could tell him the truth Only to be busy either doing nothing or consulting his Akuman. He fights anyone who suggests that the curse may be our own making. He would not let Ngarum make his pronouncement in the market place? Worse than that, he banished the poor man to Kiyung-Ndzen, As if he feared Ngarum would say something to embarrass him.
Tamfu:	I cannot believe any King

Would let this happen to his land.
The Rock would have warned us before.

Gwei: You are possibly right!
           Yet it is at times like these that the Fon
           Shows the stern veins of his authority.

Tamfu: Ours surprisingly sits there:
           Silent, sleeping, chewing and drooling!

Gwei: How do we get him to open up?

Tamfu: What do you mean open up?

Gwei: Just think about it:
           What kind of beast is it that no one has been
           able to hit?
           Is it a real beast or a beast that is more than
           beast?

Tamfu: Surely this is more than beast.

Gwei: If it is more than beast, what type of beast is
           it?

Tamfu: That sounds like a riddle!

Gwei: Exactly!
           And we are supposed to find the answer!

Tamfu: Hmmm!

Gwei: So what do you suggest?

Tamfu: I am thinking!

Gwei: Think fast, Tamfu!

Tangwa: *(A cough and Tangwa storms in)*
            Anyone in here?

Gwei: Of course Tangwa.
            Who do you want to frighten here!
            You, the only man who stays at home to eat
            his wife's fufu
            When the land is on fire!
            Stop bursting in like a wind-tossed basket and
            say something!

Tamfu: Look at him panting like one chased by a lion.

Tangwa: *(Breathlessly)*
            Stop this noise!
            You do not know how far I have traveled!
            You have no idea I was on your heels.
            I have talked with Ngarum;
            I have pleaded with him to say something
            clearly.
            He said the Rock has the Victory
            And then drove me out of his grove
            (Gwei and Tamfu exchange knowing glances)
            I came to tell you this:
            We are tired of trying to know.
            We are tired of what the elders might think.
            We have made our decision
             (Pause) We are ready!
            *(Moves towards exit and stands backing Tamfu and
            Gwei)*

Tamfu: Who is this we?

Gwei: *(Agitatedly)* What group does Tangwa lead?

Tamfu: Ngwa' of course!

Gwei: Then stop wasting the man's time!
               Give him some word?

Tamfu: Now it is confirmed, Ngarum has spoken.
               The Rock shook and the sky rumbled.
               The long battle, he said, is over
               The Rock has stood up for Bamkov!

Gwei: Except that death still takes its toll
               Which means Ngarum needs to speak again

Tamfu: That would be asking for too much.

Gwei: Then let the Fon get up and do something!

Tamfu: Something like what?

Gwei: Something the Kingdom can recognize
               For his useful effort to resolve this problem

Tamfu: Listen to you, Gwei! The Fon is as sick...

Gwei: Sick?

Tamfu: Confused!

Gwei: *(Tongue-in-cheek)* Confused like midday rain in
               the dry season!

Tamfu: What are you referring to?

Gwei: Nothing! Just let him get up!
               Let him lead!
               Instead of sitting there chewing the cord
               And drooling like a ngong dog[9] in epilepsy.

Tangwa:	*(Suddenly turning and facing Tamfu)* Lead! A Fon cannot just sit with hands between his Legs like a shy ngong dog: Suspecting everyone; Skipping in horror at every movement; And rushing for his spears at every shadow! Let him get up or we will get up!
Tamfu:	*(Turning to Gwei in shock)* Did you hear that? He is threatening!
Gwei:	Who?
Tamfu:	Who else but the Fon
Gwei:	The one who has banished our prophet? I did not hear anything like that. *(Turning knowingly towards Tangwa)* Your words are sharp like a knife! They draw blood on either blade!
Tangwa:	*(Rather dispirited and exasperated).* We are tired; very tired! We are tired of listening to elders talking; Only talking when the sun is setting on us. What do you think these young boys will grow up to remember? Corpses and carcasses they carried everyday? How can we build a land on a generation Whose hopes are shattered Like the spine of a crushed lizard? I told you before and I tell you again: The boys are ready to smoke out The beast from the depths of the forest.

(Stops abruptly realizing how intensely the others are paying attention to him)
Why are you looking at me so shocked?
I came to warn you not to relent your efforts
And to tell you to come with us tonight.
If Manjong is out of the bush, something has
to be in.
And Ngwa' is the something.
We cannot give the beast any respite!
Today, either the land adopts us
Or leave us to try it our way.
This is a warning!
(Exits in a rush)

Tamfu: *(Running after him)*
Tangwa! Tangwa! Tangwa!
Come back here!
We are not finished yet.
You have to come back.
This thing you are doing is dangerous.
We have to plan properly.

Gwei: *(Starts picking up his scabbard, horn, and spears
frantically. Then exits after him)*
On his heels, Tamfu!
Follow the strong wind.
That is the only thing able to sway the forest.
On his heels, I say!
Make sure he brings the boys for the blessing
of the land.
Run, Tamfu, run! I am behind you!
Do not let him outpace you too much.
Let us meet at the foot of Mbár Mountain.
(Fade out)

Scene Four

(Very bright moon lit night; sounds of night insects. Hunting hearth in the foreground; Ngwa[10] *vigilante troupe stands in semicircle around the hearth. Tamfu addresses them in hushed but audible voice, and sometimes rumbles out loud).*

Tamfu: Boys, the task we have tonight is not an easy one:
It is not a task for those who sleep in their beds.
It is not a task for those who doubt.
Are you ready, Ngwa?

Ngwa: Y-e-s

Tamfu: Again!

Ngwa: Y-e-s

Tamfu: Again!

Ngwa: Y-e-s

(Gwei stretches out a wooden tray from which Tamfu picks up a very short piece of wood (Sacred wood). He holds the sacred wood and scrubs its surface with a knife-like object, gathering the powder on the wood and mumbling words of ritual as he scrubs. Then he takes a few steps ahead and incants :)

Tamfu: Eh Nyuymbom![11]
Great one whose eyes never shut;
Whose ears never close!
It is you we beckon.
It is you we prod.
Turn your face Mighty Builder;

Turn your eyes toward us,
And see the wreck we have become.
We stand here under the cover of Mbár,
In the dead of night, to stir the silent bushes,
To nudge your face in this hushing wind.
You have heard our anguish;
You have seen our children die,
And our cattle disappear
All powerless before an evil that is staring us
in the eyes;
All powerless against a beast whose life has
scourged us dry.
None has been spared, needless to tell you!
We scrub this *Shinkan*[12], the sacred wood of
this land,
And gather its sacred powder in our hand:
The powder with which you blinded our
enemies!
We now blow it to you,
That you may pepper the eyes of the beast!
And deliver him to us the way you alone can.
(He blows away the dust a first time)
Pick up this night and give it your name!
Break the back of the beast.
Spill its entrails for our feast
And send its kind away
Never to appear, never to try again!
Take your powder *(Blows the powder)*
Take your powder, *(Blows the powder)*
And deliver our enemy into our hands.

(Pause)
Gwei, lead the boys to the night's assignment.
I am done.
(Exits)

Gwei: Thank you Taah[13] Tamfu.

35

Boys, you heard Tamfu, right?
The assignment is clear:
Get rid of the bug in the bed!
And deserve a cap of red feathers.

Tangwa: *(Intones Ngwa song)*
               Eh monja eh![14]

Ngwa: Heh!

Tangwa: Monja eh!

Ngwa: Heh!

Tangwa: Monja eh!

Ngwa: Heh!

Tangwa: Che wu lélé, wu lelè
               Oh ma Bah'ah, ma Gham ah
               Tati Njong eh dzem ah
Ngwa: Ho-oh!
Tangwa: Suyoh
Ngwa: Ho-oh ho –oh
Tangwa: Oh suyoh vén koy yov ah
Ngwa: Ho-oh ho –oh
Tangwa: Suyoh
Ngwa: Ho-oh
Tangwa: Oh suyoh vén koy yov ah
Ngwa: Ho-oh ho-oh
Tangwa: Suyoh
Ngwa: Ho-oh ho-ho

Tangwa: Eh monja eh!

Ngwa: Heh!

Tangwa:	Monja eh!
Ngwa:	Heh!
Tangwa:	Monja eh!
Ngwa:	Heh!
Gwei:	*(Pause and brief Silence)* Let us deploy.
Tangwa:	Step over here by the hearth, each of you Dip your three middle fingers into this bowl. Rub yourselves with that anti-sting oil. You will not slap mosquitoes off tonight However sharp the bite. You might just tell the beast where you are And he would have your entrails instead.

(The boys step over in quick succession and dip their hand in a calabash of oil and rub on the body. The leaders move slightly away and continue the conversation. Hooting of night animals and chirping of insects continue. Tamfu scoops up wood ash from the hearth, and fresh soil, mixes the two on a fresh leaf and turns his back to the hearth, his face towards the grazing ground as he adorns the forehead of each fighter)

	Quickly boys! Gwei, how many sheep did the leopard kill the other night?
Gwei:	Many.
Tangwa:	And it happened near the brook. That is where all Manjong tough men were.

Gwei: I have not understood how it could have
             happened?

Tangwa: Quickly boys!
             We saw chunks of meat and entrails in the
             morning, and where the animals were pulled
             on the grass and torn into pieces.
             Some people think it could have been hyenas:
             They are always in a pack and fight over the
             catch.

Gwei: Could it also have been lions?
             Are the boys finished?

Tangwa: Yes, Boys, as we get into action,
             Remember this:
             No one takes up position alone.
             No one changes position without another
             knowing.
             Spears could hit the wrong target.
             When you spot the beast, take your time.
             Hit the beast with a single shout.
             No long words; one word only: kpéh! [15]
             Do you hear me?
             We will melt into the undergrowth like water:
             Ten people to the left of the herd,
             Ten to the right and ten near the brook.
             Gwei and I will occupy this side of the hill.
             Tamfu will stay by the hearth with one other.
             Remember that when we knock the beast
             down,
             We cut off the legs immediately.
             If it is anyone causing this havoc,
             They will not have those legs
             Once they convert back to human.
             And you will have animal legs to prove
             That you killed a beast, not a man.

38

Let us move.

(All teams move as directed. Total silence with only night sounds coming across: Then suddenly, the cows and sheep start on a sudden stampede. Whistling indicates the boys are monitoring closely. Then another stampede follows and yet another. Tangwa's voice comes across as he jumps into the clearing).

Tangwa: *(Shouting, under his voice)* Closer everyone! *(An uneasy pause ensues)*

Gwei: *(Appears next to Tangwa, then talks in silent tones).* I think it is several of them. It does not sound like one beast.

Tangwa;   Pay attention! Did you put enough poison on my spear?

Gwei: Of course! The spears are deadly. *(As noise of the shots at the beast come the two men swing from one side of the clearing to another in readiness to hit the beast when it appears)*

Sunjo: Kpéh!!! *(Noise of running and tearing in the grass)*

Tantan: Kpéh!!! *(Noise of running and tearing in the grass in the opposite direction: Stampede follows and the bleating of sheep and desperate moos of cows is heard. Then another shout comes across)*

Binla: Kpéh!!! *(Noise of running and tearing in the grass)*
              It's here!
              (Pause)

Sunjo: Here!!! Here!!!
              (Pause)
Tantan: Here!!!

Tangwa:	*(Calling out).* Close in! Now! Everyone!!!!
Sunjo:	Kpéh!!! *(Noise of running and tearing in the grass again)* It's here! Here!!!!! *(Pause)*
Gwei:	Kpeh!!! *(Pause)*
Tantan:	Here!!!
Tangwa:	*(Calling out).* Close in quickly!

(Gradual drop in noise as stampede subsides, followed by a longer spell of silence. Cock-crows: The entire Ngwa' appears in bright moonlight on the clearing. A few dead sheep lie in front; intermittent bleating goes on as the herd tries to regain comfort. Four men can be seen breathing heavily).

Gwei:	Watch out. He can pounce at any time! *(Pause, murmurs; then gradually loud talking resumes)*
Tangwa:	Come around everyone. It seems we scared the beast away instead. I think there are several of them. The way he appears all over the place tells me that it is several of them. I am not sure he was hit.
Gwei:	A single scratch will end him.
Tangwa:	Be careful! The beast could be up in the tree.
Gwei:	Stop frightening people!

40

Tangwa: I am not!

Gwei: If the beast could be everywhere, then how do
            we even make progress?

Tangwa: I just meant to caution us not to talk loudly.
            Let us get back into the thicket and wait for
            another chance. He could still appear.

Gwei: So what do you think this is?

Tangwa: What do you mean?

Gwei: How many leopards are there?

Tangwa: One lead leopard. Seems to be a female!

Gwei: How many others with her?

Tangwa: How would I know?

Gwei: You are TAV-NGWA![16]

Tangwa: Several others; possibly with cobs! From the
            way she hunts and the droppings she leaves
            behind, it must be a female.

Gwei: Could it be that these are people just out to
            destroy this land? I have never heard of
            leopards that no one has been able to even
            wound with a spear after so much hunting.
            Yet the devastation they leave behind is so
            heavy.

Tangwa: I am not sure this one has gone away. It must
            have pounced on the sheep and then realized
            that we were too close, so it dropped the meat

and took off.

Tangwa: For it to drop the kill means it must have
            smelt danger, very close.
            If it was a single person, the beast would have
            faced him!

Gwei: Yes, it surely realized that we were a crowd.
(Pause)
            Is it possible it might still come back?

Tangwa: If it is still hungry. Leopards have very little
            tolerance for hunger.
            Hunger makes the beast less cautious and very
            dangerous too, especially if it is a female and
            has cobs. Now let us move those who went to
            the brook up here. You will be here guarding
            the dead sheep. It is a good trap.
            (To the troupe) All of you to my right move to
            the right of the herd. All on my left move near
            the plantain farm. Watch out for each other as
            you shoot.
            Look over there under the sky. That is day
            cracking its way through. That means this
            round will be a very short one. Tamfu is
            waiting to hear from us. Let us move.

(They start moving into the thicket; then rumbles come off from the
brook side of the herd; then a stampede follows amidst raised voices
echoing in quick succession. They continue moving in attack from one
direction to the other as frantic voices call. Tangwa and Gwei rush from
end to end as voices and stampede dictate)

Sunjo: Watch the direction of the running herd!

Tantan: Can't see him?

Binla:	I see only cattle!
Tantan:	Look down. The legs!
Binla:	Can't see. It's dark!
Sunjo:	Bend down!
Binla:	Nothing on the ground!
Tantan:	Just legs!
Sunjo:	The one with open space around it!
Tantan:	It's H-e-r-e!
Binla:	Here... Here!
Sunjo:	Surround the herd! Towards the hearth!
Tantan:	F-a-s-t!
Binla:	F-a-s-t!
Tantan:	P-u-s-h!
Binla:	R-u-s-h!

(Gwei and Tangwa gird up in readiness as the stampede heads towards them. Daylight is all over)

Gwei:	I will hold this section!
Tangwa:	Me here! Watch your back.
Gwei:	What?

Tangwa:	The beast could be sneaky!
Gwei:	I hear the herd stomping toward us!
Tangwa:	Ready?
Gwei:	Ready!
Tangwa:	No noise! *(Pause)*
Gwei:	Who'll watch the legs?
Tangwa:	You!
Gwei:	Sure?
Tangwa:	Down on your belly!
Gwei:	If he jumps on me?
Tangwa:	I'll jump on him!
Gwei:	My head would be gone!
Tangwa:	And the beast too!
Gwei:	That is suicide for me!
Tangwa:	No! You'll fight him too as I attack from the back!
Gwei:	Dangerous!
Tangwa:	You should have stayed home then!
Gwei:	They are here!

Tangwa: Get down!

(The stampede increases in intensity and rumbles off louder and louder. A heavy leopard snarl issues from behind Gwei. Gwei flattens on the ground as Tangwa aims and shoots a spear. He misses. The leopard's growling gets louder as it approaches Gwei slowly and steadily with a drooling mouth. Its eye catches Tangwa as he aims the next spear. Before he releases it, the Leopard skips smartly away. The stampede drops to silence. Tangwa runs and tears around to further scare the beast away; then moves over and tries to get Gwei up on his feet).

Tangwa: *(Frantically)*
                Get up on your legs Taah Gwei! Get up!

Gwei: *(Breathless and dazed)*
                Who are you, trying to wake up a spirit?

Tangwa: Gwei, it's me, Tangwa!

Gwei: You too came with me to the spirit world?

Tangwa: No, Gwei, you are here!

Gwei: Yes we are here. How come?

Tangwa: Because we were here together!

Gwei: That was before the Leopard came!

Tangwa: And when it came you did what you were
                supposed to do.

Gwei: No. I was not supposed to!
Tangwa: Did you want to stay up and fight him?

Gwei: Yes!

45

Tangwa:	You surprise me!
Gwei:	How?
Tangwa:	Because you have forgotten the rules
Gwei:	What is the use remembering the rules in the land of the dead!
Tangwa:	*(Angrily)* Will you stop it! You are not dead!
Gwei:	How can the land of the dead be so real?
Tangwa:	Because it is not the land of the dead.
Gwei:	Then what is it?
Tangwa:	The land of the living!
Gwei:	You mean I am living?
Tangwa:	Yes!
Gwei:	How is that possible?
Tangwa:	Because nothing killed you
Gwei:	But…the Leopard! The growl and the fangs…!
Tangwa:	Then you went flat!
Gwei:	Yes…!
Tangwa:	That means respect for the beast!

Gwei:	And he left?
Tangwa:	Not exactly!
Gwei:	*(Tearfully)* So he mauled me up then!
Tangwa:	No!
Gwei:	What happened?
Tangwa:	My first spear missed him!
Gwei:	*(Tearfully)* Then he mauled me! You let him tear my body into pieces!
Tangwa:	No! You want me to prove?
Gwei:	Yes
Tangwa:	Give me your arm. No, the right one! *(Pulls out a hunting knife)*
Gwei:	What do you want to do?
Tangwa:	If you are spirit, you should feel no pain.
Gwei:	But if you are spirit too?
Tangwa:	At least I know I am not.
Gwei:	No, you are. And you are fooling me!
Tangwa:	What use is it for me to be fooling you?
Gwei:	How would I know!

Tangwa: How can you not know! Now lie still.

(Harvests some herbs from around them, selects and test twist them for juice. Realizes an abundance of juice; then kneels over Gwei and starts applying)

Open your mouth Taah Gwei!
Open it!
Yes, wider.
(Squeezes; Gwei spits out some of the juice)
Swallow it Gwei!
This is medication to calm your nerves.
(Squeezes more and more)
Swallow the juice, and then relax.
(The rest of the party joins them. Gwei is lying in semi-sleep from the effect of the juice.)
Someone run to the hearth and call Tamfu for me! Sunjo, hurry!

Tantan: *(As he is coming in)*
What happened to Taah Gwei?

Binla: *(As he is coming in)*
Did the beast attack him?

Tantan: What happened? Is he breathing?

Tangwa: Keep quiet all of you! I have sent for Tamfu
Let us wait for him to come.

Binla: Luckily he is not hurt on the body.

Tangwa: Wait for Tamfu to come.

Tantan: I always thought Taah Gwei would not take advice.
This is what comes from shutting your ears!

48

Tangwa: Oh you shut your mouth!

Binla: But the man is almost dead, Bah[17] Tangwa.
             How can we afford to say nothing?

Tangwa: And if he is dying, will that bring him back?

Binla: Well, no, but it will help us as we think about
             him.

Tangwa: *(Quietly)* You are talking to his hearing. Do not
             be surprised if he repeats the same thing and
             swear that he saw the people who said it in
             the spirit world.

Tantan: He did? Is that what he was saying? Spirit
             world?

Tangwa: Shut up, young man!

             (Tamfu enters followed by Sunjo)

Tamfu: Who is talking about the spirit world here!
             That kind of talk must stop immediately!
             (Kneeling down near Gwei) Now where are we,
             Tangwa?

Tangwa: He is almost totally asleep now, but that is
             from the herbs I squeezed into his mouth. I
             am not sure what next to do. He lost his mind
             completely when the leopard appeared right
             behind him as he lay on the ground facing the
             opposite direction. I missed the beast with the
             first spear. And it ran away before I could try
             the second. Then after, Gwei never recovered.

For him, he was already in the jaws of the beast and only his spirit could be speaking. When I squeezed the juice into his mouth, he went into this kind of sleep. That is why I called you. I do not know what to do at this point. I thought you might have your Mfuh' bag[18].

(Tamfu pulls out his short bull horn from the raffia handbag and shakes out some medication from it; robs it in front of Gwei's nostrils. Suddenly, Gwei starts sniffing loudly and loudly. Then Tamfu motions everyone to clear away into the nearby brushes. Gwei sniffs louder and wakes up with eyes red and dripping with tears. He grabs his spears and scabbards and tumbles down; then gathers himself up only to try a few steps like a drunkard and crash into one little heap. He pulls himself together, gets up gradually and lets out a loud Mfuh shout; Tangwa answers from behind the thicket. They get into Ngwa song. Tamfu and the rest of the vigilante sing the song. As the song dies down, Tamfu speaks.)

Tamfu: Gwei, lead the way out.

Gwei: Me? Way out to where?

Tamfu: Home.

Gwei: I am not going home.

Tamfu: Where are you going?

Gwei: Kifeh

Tamfu: What for?

Gwei: What day is today?

Tamfu: Ntangrin.[19]

Gwei: And you want me to go back home on
             Ntangrin?

Tamfu: You came here from your house. I would
             expect you to return to your house.

Gwei: I am going to the market.

Tamfu: Without even a rat in your bag! What are you
             going to sell?

Gwei: Nothing.

Tamfu: What are you going to buy?

Gwei: Nothing!

Tamfu: You are going to the market: Nothing to sell;
             nothing to buy. May be you you are going to
             steal.

Gwei: Tamfu, you surprise me sometimes. How
             does a man stay home on market day?

Tamfu: Well, tomorrow is Kavi, the market day in
             Nkim-mbo. It seems to me you will just
             continue to that one from Kifeh
             .

Gwei: Tamfu, I am not nursing a baby at home, and
             there is enough for my wife and those in the
             house to eat. Now, stay out of this! *(Picks up
             his bag, wipes his buttocks and is about to leave. Then
             he turns and faces Tamfu and the rest of the troupe
             again)* All of you stay out of this. Do you hear
             me? *(Exits)*

ACT TWO

Scene One

(Sunny and comfortably breezy day: Corn beer shed in the market. Kibong, a middle aged lady is sitting at the door. A big pot from which she serves corn beer into bowls, stands at the back corner. Very clean calabash bowls are neatly packed face-down on a bamboo bench along the wall. The floor is watered swept; market noise in the background; Gwei walks in tired and Kibong smiles broadly when she notices him.)

Kibong: Taah Gwei! I knew it would be you. I was afraid you might not be able to open my market[20] today.

Gwei: It does not matter how tired I am...

Kibong: Or how dirty...

Gwei: *(Checks his clothes)* Stop that kind of talk, will you.

Kibong: I did not mean harm. Only joking!

Gwei: Of course I knew that. As I was saying, the Ntangrin[21] I do not appear at this door, will be the one that announces my death.

Kibong: How is my sister today? Lukong the palm wine tapper said yesterday that she told him you have been away on the errand of the land

Gwei: Yes, I was. I have not gone back home yet.

Kibong: *(Surprised)* I know the beast is not letting up, but why have you not

returned home at least for a short while? Is that how you treat my sister?

Gwei: Do not start the day like this. Take. *(Throws some money on the floor)* Now that I have opened the door to your market, can I start with my bonus bowl of Nkáng?[22]

Kibong: Anytime. But tell me why you have not returned home yet, Taah Gwei. If there is anything with my sister, we can always fix it.

Gwei: None at all. My errands took me to Ntangrin, and I could not begin to dangle myself home when today is market day.

Kibong: Only that?

Gwei: Only that!

Kibong: That means you have not eaten anything yet.

Gwei: You guessed right.

Kibong: Rush home and bathe. The children are at home, and will get you something to eat before you come back.

Gwei: Not before I have finished this one bowl.

Kibong: *(Notices someone coming at a distance)* Who is that like your friend?

Gwei: Who?

Kibong: You know who. Tell him if he wants another wife, he should go give palm wine to a lineage head[23]. I am not going to be bothered with him anymore.

Gwei: Both of you are like a pot of bad soup, its coat of oil swinging stubbornly on top from pot jaw to pot jaw.

Kibong: Not with his dancing all over the place! What kind of man is it that wants to marry every woman he meets?

Gwei: A genuine man!

Kibong: A what?

Gwei: A true man!

Kibong: True man! True like a dirty pot! Rubbish!

Gwei: At least you know who he is before getting involved with him.

Kibong: Who do you think would want the head ache? Me?

Gwei: If you choose to.

Kibong: Don't you start trying to build his bridges.

Gwei;   I am not, but there is something about him that I most admire.
           He tells you what he shows you about himself. You are no more in fear that you could ever be deceived. That is him. You take it or leave it.

Kibong:	That I agree. But no one enters a river when they know they will drown.
Gwei:	So leave those who can swim to wallow in the river.
Kibong:	He is deep and swift! He is for swimmers!
Gwei:	Just leave the poor man alone then.
Kibong:	Who is complaining about him?
Gwei:	Seems you are not!
Kibong:	Stop trying to play tricks on me.
Gwei:	Who is playing tricks on whom?
Kibong:	If you had gone to clean up, we would not be on this now.
Gwei:	Who knows? It could have been worse.
Kibong:	Worse? What do you mean?
Gwei:	Nothing!
	(Pause as Tangwa approaches)
Tangwa:	Taah Gwei, are you done with the first bowl already?
Gwei:	I thought market days were only for me.
Tangwa:	You are not referring to the incident earlier today, are you?

Gwei: Why should I not?

Tangwa: You did not see my mouth open, or even hear a cough from me, did you?

Gwei: No, but what is the difference?

Kibong: What happened earlier?

Tangwa: You don't need to know.

Kibong;   I was not talking to you!

Tangwa: Is that how you welcome me into your shed?

Kibong: Who asked you to come?

Tangwa: Did someone have to?

Kibong: *(Ignores him, but still seems furious)* Yes!

Tangwa: I thought this was a shed in the market, and today is Ntangrin

Kibong: There are other sheds in this market

Tangwa: How many sheds belong to women whose parents will drink our palm wine?

Gwei: I thought you were marrying all the women you see!

Kibong: You keep your mouth out of this Taah Gwei!

Tangwa: Why should he? If you speak from both sides of the mouth, your words will haunt you as soon as they come out of your mouth.

Kibong: Leave my brother out of this, Tangwa.
            (Mumbles scornfully at Tangwa) "Words will
            haunt you as soon as they come out."

Tangwa: Nothing to drink? Even if you want to bring
            down rain on me, aren't you going to offer me
            something to drink first?

Kibong: This is not my house. This is a shed in the
            market, and if you do not have money, you
            cannot have a drink.

Tangwa: Taah Gwei, if you turn your back on me on
            this one, darkness will swallow me at noon.[24]

Gwei: I allow you to come wooing in my house and
            then I give you a drink in addition?

Tangwa: This is not your house Taah Gwei. This is a
            shed in the market. *(Grabbing Gwei's bowl)* And
            by the way, what is a drink between friends?

Gwei: That bowl you are holding means double
            bride price.

Kibong: That is your own bride price, not mine.

Gwei: *(Impatient with Kibong)* Stop wasting our time,
            Kibong. You either want the man, or you do
            not. You cannot go ahead having children
            with a man whom you claim is not good
            enough for you to marry. What is the use?
            Two children with the same man, and yet
            from day one, he has never been good enough
            to be your husband?

59

Kibong:	Who wants to bury himself in this prison? I will take care of my children and send all of them to school from this small shed. I cannot bring Tangwa with all his trouble and poverty to ruin the plans I have for them.
Tangwa:	*(Agitated)* Stop her now before she angers me further. Stop her Taah Gwei! She is challenging my manhood!
Gwei:	Challenging your manhood with what Tangwa? You have two children with her and a line of them in your house to prove yourself.
Tangwa:	Why is she implying that I cannot raise my children? Why is she saying I cannot be a good father?
Gwei:	And you are getting angry over that? You should be happy she is even helping you to raise them.
Tangwa:	*(Visibly frustrated and angry)* You this weakling! How dare you insult me? Look at you quivering like a frost bitten reed early today in the face of a challenge.
Gwei:	Is that how you want to come? You want to go there? *(Pulls out his machete)* You want to see who the man is between us?
Tangwa:	Flat like the soil itself in the face of a leopard and you dare to challenge my manhood?
Gwei:	If I open my mouth again, you will be on your way to Mbohlah![25]

Kibong: You men! Behave like the problem solvers
            that you are. Sit down both of you! Sit down!
            This is my shed, and you have to listen to me
            or leave. *(Fills a bowl and puts it on the bamboo
            table in front of the men.)* You share this! Don't
            behave like filthy rats that have no idea how
            sacred blood is.

Gwei: I hope you know that he started it.

Tangwa: Who? You started it!

Gwei: No, you did!

Tangwa: You did!

Gwei: You did!

Tangwa: You did!

Gwei: You did!

Kibong: Enough! Enough you two! Now both of you
            sit down! Men behaving worse than children!

*(They regain their seats; tensions subside with an uneasy pause; then
Kibong starts almost distractedly, and avoiding the men's faces. As she
speaks, the men gaze at each other as if to say, how could you have told
her all this.)*

Kibong: What happened between the two of you early
            today is a true test of manhood and honesty.
            Imagine that even at this hour, it still stirs up
            so much pain and anger.

Gwei:	*(Rather shocked and dismayed)*. So Tangwa had been here already? He told you all that already. Alright! And now he is pretending as if …
Tangwa:	Been here already doing what? If your courage leaks like a badly thatched roof, do not blame your guilt on someone saying anything to the lady.
Gwei:	So my courage leaks! That is what you concluded. That is your impression of me. This very Gwei and you call him weak!
Tangwa:	I do not know what you are talking about. The woman is only trying to play us like a cat.
Gwei:	Which woman? The one who a few moments ago was telling us that we are behaving worse than children?
Tangwa:	Be careful what you tell her. You might just tell her too much.
Gwei:	That is my sister you are talking about.
Tangwa:	No, that is your sister IN-LAW
Gwei:	Stop this in-lawfulness. A sister is a sister!
Tangwa:	No!
Gwei:	What?
Tangwa:	I say no! I cannot carry palm wine to your house,[26] if I wanted her, can I?

Gwei: You think if you bring it, I will not drink?

Tangwa: On whose count will you drink?

Gwei: On my useful guardianship!

Tangwa: That is as if I bought you a bowl of Nkáng on
            market day!

Gwei: And then I point you to the right direction.

Tangwa: Now you see! There is a right direction! And I
            could know it from somewhere else.

Gwei: Why look up in the ceiling for what is on the
            floor. I am here and I know it. So just ask me,
            but do it right, and you'll be on the way.
            Kibong, don't sigh like that. This is about you.

Kibong: You think this idiot Tangwa is a fool? He is
            very clever.

Gwei: Stop this Tangwa thing and tell me mother
            trickster,[27] how is it that you quell a fire only
            to ignite it with another dry leaf?[28]

Kibong: That is when I want to know how naked you
            men are.

Gwei: Now that you have found where our balls are
            dangling, can you go carry your sister out of a
            weakling's house?

Kibong: Stop that Gwei! Stop it.

Gwei: Answer me: Will you go pack her out of a
            weakling's house or will you not?

Kibong: He-e-e-i! Pack you out of my sister's house?
             Of course I could do it anytime.

Gwei: By the time I get home tonight, make sure
             you have finished your task because I will get
             back like a lion.

Tangwa: Oh shut up! What lion? Flat on the ground
             and almost out of breath! And you think you
             will get anywhere like a hero! Heroism of the
             dogs!

Gwei: I did not choose to lie down; you suggested
             like the master hunter, that I should. And it
             worked. You should be ashamed for failing to
             even hit the beast standing there in front of
             you. And you call yourself a master hunter.
             TAV-NGWA my head![29]

Tangwa: Who turned vegetable? Who thought he was
             dead; you or I? Look at you, shivering little
             man!

Gwei: I have had it. But I am not going to insult my
             sister here by tearing you down right away.

Kibong: Slow down, you men. What I gather is that
             both of you faced the beast, and Gwei went
             flat on his stomach and passed out. But
             Tangwa who was on his two legs and carrying
             his full armor could not even shoot the beast,
             let alone kill it.

Gwei:	And that is not all, he was happy he scared it away. We went there to kill that beast, not to scare it away. The people are still in danger, all because Tangwa let the beast walk away, and he is here making noise.
Kibong:	My customers are not pouring in because of the two of you. So get up and leave!
Tangwa:	*(Beating his chest)* I am not leaving. Who ever is father to your children should come and sit on my seat. Nonsense!
Gwei:	I have to go throw water on my body, then come back to get some meat for Lantir and the children, before I start singing myself down home.
Kibong;	And you, what are you still doing sitting here?
Tangwa:	Now don't start that your nonsense again!
Gwei:	If you cannot marry the man, but keep bearing his children, then allow the man to at least sit.
Kibong:	Bearing whose children? MY children, not his!
Gwei:	Oh, oh! I am out and on my way. You can tear him and eat like meat. That is up to you. *(Exit, and fade out)*

Scene Two

(Moonlit night: Gwei sings along the road, shouting greetings to all those with houses by the road-side as he treks by. From time to time, the eyes of an animal flash quickly by as it crosses the road. Gwei sounds a little tipsy, but sure of foot)

Gwei: *(Sings as he walks along; then calls out)*
Tabiy of Shiy! Gwei greets you and the family!
What drove you away from the market, Tabiy?
Did you get a new bride? Well, snore
comfortably, and don't leave any chances,
Tabiy. Twins don't come easy!
(Sings along)

Uu Oh Lamari wo Mbohtong oh
Aah ho-ho-ho
Uu Oh oh oh Mbaah-mban oh
Aah ho-ho-ho
Wir loh ban wan-oh wu nen toy fishong
Oh uuh ho-ho-ho

(Calls out)
Bongaman of Kilán ké Nyuy! Gwei greets
you!
Either I am traveling too late or you went to
bed too early. Well, give us only children,
Bongaman: boys and girls!
(Sings along)

Lamari óh-oh òh
Lam oh len áh ah àh
Ho-hó-ho, ho-hó-ho
Foh moh m'du wira ka Manjong keh' ku
Hò-ho-hó, ho-hó-ho-hó-ho

(Calls out)

66

Johji of Ngewir, no more palm wine for the lonely passerby? *(Pause)* Silence and darkness in your house tell me you had too much to drink already. I will see you tomorrow after you inspect your traps. We will break a kola nut.

(Sings along)

Hóyò-hóyoh hóyò-ho
Hayo–hóyòh hayo-ho
Sa wiy siyla shah lavoh
Nginyam siy ni kum toy oh

(Calls out)

Inusa Verla of Ngewirr. Tell me why I should not call your grandfather, Tabesov by name, if you can be sleeping now. Who is guarding the Rock of God, Inusa if you are asleep? Twelve children already, you cannot be troubling that poor mother of twins anymore. Abai Inusa, even if your knife is still as sharp as it was yesterday, just let that poor woman sleep. But if the hunger is hers, Inusa, forgive me, but make sure you take the next child to Tabesov. That one is his own to raise, after all he got the wife for you.

(Sings along, sounding off the Manjong drum verbally)

(Two shiny dots ahead of him indicate that a beast might be coming directly at him from the opposite direction. Gwei stops briefly; then it growls and the growling tells him it is a leopard. He readies his spear and pulls out the machete. The growling grows bigger and more frightening. Then Gwei issues a loud warning)

I am not sure who you are, but you are facing Gwei Bamkov.

If you are man enough, wear the right coat
and talk to me, man to man.
If you are beast, count your jaw bones
crushed and entrails food for birds.
No animal meets these Manjong spears and
machetes and escapes whole.
Whoever you are, realize we are at the
threshold of the Rock of God.

*(Animal growling resumes and becomes intense. Gwei issues Manjong
shouts, in quick succession indicating both danger and urgency.)*
Oh uuuuh, Oh uuuuh, oh uuuuh!
Oh uuuuh, Oh uuuuh, oh uuuuh!

*(The eyes continue moving towards Gwei; then all of a sudden, they
start moving in very fast zig-zag. Gwei releases a spear, and shouts as
the animal slows and anguish comes from the howling of the beast.
Then the flashing eyes start coming in the air like a pair of touch lights
again. Gwei issues another Manjong shout as he extends his arm to
strike with the machete. Loud successive bang and crash noises indicate
head-on collision with the beast; then cries of anguish and pain woven
in the howling of the beast indicate that Gwei and the beast are
tangled up. Rumbling noises follow; then a long desperate groan from
the beast and a loud cry of pain from Gwei. And silence!)*

Scene Three

(Kavi: day after Kifeh market day. Rainy season morning; bright and sunny on the green grass cover. Two women are about to leave the house when a Nwerong masquerade approaches, pulling along a bamboo pole. It stops, scans the surroundings from left to right, puts hand over forehead for a piercing look into the house and then proceeds. The masquerade is accompanied by one bare-footed middle-aged man. The women hide behind the door and watch. As soon as Nwerong clunkers along with the bamboo pole, the ladies surface.)

Lantir: *(Panting)* You see what I was telling you? You see what I have been trying to explain?

Befeh: It is shocking. There is no word to describe it.

Lantir: And yet he does not listen. What am I going to do with him? He has ears but does not hear.

Befeh: Are you sure they still want him to serve?

Lantir: Yes, I am sure. They had chosen him as the replacement for his grand father who served in the palace for over nine years.

Befeh: Nine years of apprenticeship or nine years of service as a page?

Lantir: What is the difference? You are taken there when you are still a very young boy. Then you grow up there learning how to serve and guard the Fon and the palace.

Befeh: What I was referring to is whether he spent nine years of service after the nine years of apprenticeship.

Lantir:	I have not heard of anyone who did two separate nines. Any way, by the end of the first year, the boy thinks only of the palace and all that goes on around there.
Befeh:	Is it not already late for him to embark on a nine-year term of service in the palace? He is a grown man with family. Besides, he is old.
Lantir:	That is what we thought! We thought that if we avoided them for a number of years, age alone would disqualify him. But you have seen Nwerong here yourself.
Befeh:	But I have not heard that Nwerong arrested anyone and took them to the palace of late. I don't believe they could have been here to capture him like game.
Lantir:	I don't care how they operate. I just know they want the father of my children. I just don't want them around.
Befeh:	Could it be something else?
Lantir:	What else? Have you ever seen a chick screaming for cover for no reason? There must be a hawk hovering above.
Befeh:	Have you heard from him?
Lantir:	Yes and no! Tangwa's son, Lavran, said he and Tangwa were drinking Nkáng at my sister's shed yesterday at the Kifeh market. He said Gwei said he would be leaving for home before nightfall.

Befeh:	And he is not here by now. I think he might have stayed overnight at your sister's house to start the trip early in the morning.
Lantir:	Very unlikely. When he is on his two feet, my children's father thinks he can brave anything – night, animal or man.
Befeh:	You mean...heh! No, he could not have tried traveling in the night. The leopard has been ravaging children and cattle around the foot of Tan[30] so much that it would be stupid for anyone to trek down that road alone even in bright moon light.
Lantir:	But that is the man I have. And he does not walk quietly on market days. He sings all the way home. It is like taunting every beast in the bush.
Befeh:	Why don't you complain to Tamfu. He would at least be able to give some useful information.
Lantir:	Who? Tamfu? Is he not one of those quietly plotting behind my husband? I am not talking to him for any reason.
Befeh:	Oh, so you had talked to him about it already!
Lantir:	No! But why has he never called me to discuss the matter? Can you imagine that he has been aware of all this and yet kept his lips tight?

Befeh:	You have never addressed the matter to him, but you know that he is against your husband. How do you know that for sure?
Lantir:	If you have lived in this Bamkov as long as I have, you would understand what I am saying. If you have known him as much as I have, you would understand what I am saying.

(Voice can be heard faintly making an announcement.)

Befeh:	Whose voice is that? And why is he making an announcement? *(Mumbles after listening keenly)* Strange that it is a different person other than Gwei making the announcement.
Lantir:	Whatever he is announcing, I am not going to be a part of it.
Befeh:	How can you say that? The announcement does not have to be something about the palace or Nwerong. Besides, announcements are made only when there are serious things the people need to know.
Lantir:	I have been in this place long enough to know the difference. *(Voice is clearer and continuously making the announcement. Lantir sees Tamfu almost nearing her house and begins to pull the friend inside urgently)* That is him coming towards this house. We must get in now and shut the door!
Befeh:	He is not a lion. We cannot be running away from him in that way. We have to wait here until he says what he has to say.

Lantir: And what does he want to say? Nothing! I tell
               you, nothing!

Befeh: If it is nothing, then let us listen to it first.

Lantir: You want to stay? Alright, you stay, but I am
               going in right now.

Befeh: Why, Lantir? Announcements of this nature
               are important because they carry something
               for the entire community.

Lantir: *(Very worked up)* When elders and rulers plot
               against defenseless families, you call it
               something good for the entire community?
               He is coming here from a house where he ate
               his wife's corn-fufu. What about Gwei?
               *(Tamfu is now very audible and his voice overcomes
               the entire surrounding)*

Tamfu: The Fon, our Fon, is on the river banks
               To feast with his own eyes the demise of our
               pain.
               The Leopard is in pieces.
               The beast has been beaten.
               Life has returned to the land
               And the Fon is summoning all of us.
               Everyone: man, woman and child,
               The Fon summons you to come see him
               Thatch our heads with red feathers.
               What tore us down has been torn down!
               What trashed our sleep has been trashed.
               The Fon is waiting with a smile!
               The smile of a groom on his nuptial night!
               Everybody, man, woman and child
               Hurry over to the river banks
               And see the leopard:

Its coat in shreds,
Its limbs shattered;
Its eyes a yawning socket;
Its' claws food for insects;
Its mane a thatch for your roofs;
And you can feed your dogs with its entrails
Because Gwei, your Gwei, has brought the
beast down!
In one night Gwei hacked down our darkness!
In one night Gwei brought us a song!
Yekong Lantir, your cold nights have brought
us a glowing log.
Your cold days have won the kingdom its
warm rays!
Today, your sunbath just started!
All of you hurry to the banks of the river!
Join the Fon and for the first time see the
entrails of a Leopard.
Empty your homes of everyone and let us
hold a leopard watch.
Leopard-watch is going on as we speak.
All you children of this land,
Join your kingdom to feast on your threat!
Be there to wear your crown:
Your crown of red feathers.
(Silent for a brief moment. No other sound is heard)
I am on my way. *(Exits)*
*(As he disappears Lantir and Befeh appear. Lantir is
dressed as if in readiness for confrontation. Lantir is
ahead and carries a club on the shoulder. Befeh follows
rather reluctantly.)*

Lantir: *(Panting and agitated through out the scene.)* You
have to hurry!
These people are up to something. We cannot
close our eyes for one
        moment. They'll sweep us away!

74

Befeh: Are you doing the right thing?

Lantir: Why?

Befeh: Because Tamfu cannot be summoning the
            land to the presence of the
            Fon just to have your husband pronounced
            apprentice page in the palace.

Lantir: That is exactly the issue. Just because they
            know they can hide it, they
            wrap it in a big event, or one that they have
            made to sound so big.

Befeh: You mean the Fon would come all the way
            from the palace for something as small as
            securing a page for the palace? Has a Fon ever
            done that?

Lantir: But do you believe this thing about the
            leopard? Whoever heard of something like
            that?

Befeh: What he has said is that we all need to be
            there because the Fon is honoring your
            husband. He has even said that you and your
            children have been honored forever in this
            land. Instead of dressing up this way, wear
            your Ceremonial gowns and let us take our
            cups along for a good drink.

Lantir: Wear gowns? Ceremony? Honor? You do not
            seem to understand even the ground on
            which you are standing!

Befeh: I think you do not totally understand the
            ground on which you stand.

75

Lantir:	What? I have not seen my man at home for how many days now?
Befeh:	But that does not mean that he cannot do something worthy of honor. Is that not why he went to the bush in the first place?
Lantir:	You do not understand!
Befeh:	No, YOU do not understand!
Lantir:	Whether it is the palace or red feather, it is the same. Lineage heads will start competing to fill his house with wives
Befeh:	I see. So that is your problem!
Lantir:	Only part of the problem!
Befeh:	Then we have a difficult battle ahead of us.
Lantir:	Why?
Befeh:	How can you fight something that big?
Lantir:	How big is it?
Befeh:	Imagine all the lineage heads in the whole kingdom; imagine the power of the palace and all the people who believe the red feather is also their honor. How do you fight all these people?
Lantir:	By seizing my husband from their hands!

Befeh:	How will you do that? His achievement has changed him. He is now a bigger figure; when he will speak, people will listen. He is possibly enjoying every moment of the whole thing now. How then can you seize him from their hands?
Lantir:	I think you are mad!
Befeh:	No, I think you are mad!
Lantir:	Have you been sent by them? How can you change all of a sudden?
Befeh:	Changed? You have! Be careful Lantir, otherwise you will start chasing your shadow[31] very soon.
Lantir:	You still think I am mad? Just wait and see!
Befeh:	I will wait here.
Lantir:	No, you will come with me. *(Pulling her)* Let us go!
Befeh:	Sure! Let us go and join the throng at the leopard watch.
Lantir:	There will be no leopard watch.
Befeh:	What ?
Lantir:	The hurricane will turn the place up-side-down!
Befeh:	Where will it come from; you?

Lantir: You have not seen something yet!

Befeh: Calm down Lantir! You do not seem to see
              how impracticable what you are trying to do
              is.

Lantir: Impracticable? I told you to wait and see.

Befeh: And I told you that I would wait right here!

Lantir: But I need someone to work with!

Befeh: There is no one to work on a crazy plan like
              this. There is nothing in what you are saying
              apart from just fear; fear that there may be a
              cooked up plan by the palace disguised in
              some form.

Lantir: You think there is none; I think there is one!

Befeh: Oh stop this madness Lantir! Our women's
              dance, Chong, has surely gathered over there
              by now. And the women are surely looking
              forward to seeing you because you provided
              your husband all the support to do this. Tell
              me just how you will ignore such warmth to
              start a fight. It is not possible, and I am asking
              you to stop this madness. I am going ahead!

Lantir: *(Restraining her)* No, you cannot!

Befeh: Why not?

Lantir: You cannot leave me here alone!

Befeh: I am not leaving you here alone!

78

Lantir:	Did anyone ever hear such madness!
Befeh:	What madness?
Lantir:	Leaving me here and refusing you are doing exactly that!
Befeh:	Again, I am not leaving you here alone!
Lantir:	What are you doing?
Befeh:	I am leaving you to your plan!
Lantir:	Ohoh! So I am going to be alone?
Befeh:	If you do not join the women and the rest of the people!
Lantir:	No, you cannot leave?
Befeh:	I am certainly!
Lantir:	Then wait for me!
Befeh:	We cannot enter there together if you are dressed like this.
Lantir:	Like what?
Befeh:	Like this! *(Pointing to her costume)*
Lantir:	How am I dressed?
Befeh:	For war!
Lantir:	But I am going for war!

Befeh:	Then you will get there alone!
Lantir:	It is no one else's husband but mine.
Befeh:	He is now Gwei Fon[32]. What will you do to change it?
Lantir:	Get him out and into his house.
Befeh:	Where Nwerong, Manjong and the palace can still get to him whenever they want.
Lantir:	Why are you doing this to me Befeh?
Befeh:	I am asking myself why you are doing this to me and your family; why you are doing this to the land? The kingdom has been festering from devastation caused by the leopard. And now that the leopard is dead, all you see are your personal problems. I have to leave. I cannot be late just because I am trying to make you happy.
Lantir:	That is a good reason to be here with me.
Befeh:	But you do not want to be happy! I do not have time to waste. *(Seizes herself and runs out)*
Lantir:	Let me get my machete, hoe, and knife, and if Gwei has any spare spear, I should carry that along too. Today is today! Leopard watch or whatever they call it will end up in smoke today. *(Runs into the house and picks up tools, then runs back and calls out for Befeh)* Befeh! Befeh! Where are you? You have decided to join ranks with those plotting the demise of my household? You have finally

decided to fall prey to the same decease that is eating household upon household in this land? I want my husband home not somewhere in the palace no matter the harvest of red feathers he may bring.

(Scampering around as if for some more fighting tools, then discovering she does not need anything else, she calls after the friend) Befeh, wait for me! Wait Befeh! But I tell you that no matter what all of you say, today will be today! *(Runs out)*

Scene Four

(Banks of the Kiléy Báh River: Manjong is in full gear dancing and singing. On the foreground is a flat rock on which lies Gwei on one side and a shattered Leopard on another side. Manjong medicine experts are trying to revive Gwei. Gwei starts waking up as drumming and singing rise to a sudden high. Gwei is lifted and taken out by a few hefty Manjong warriors. Women and men dancers form a half circle over the leopard. His Majesty the Fon makes his entrance amidst ululations and jubilation. Then a shout from Tamfu brings silence in the crowd)

Tamfu: Manjong, kwéh! Be quiet now and listen!
                Chong and you mothers and princesses, listen!
                It is time to open our ears.
                It is time to hear the lion speak!
                Let not a toe rustle the sand underfoot;
                Let not a bird chirp now.
                It is time!

                Your Majesty, here are your people
                Here stands Manjong;
                Here stands Chong
                On the foot of Tan.
                Here your plains are calmed
                By the murmurs of the river
                On its tumble from the spine of the hill,
                Washing clean this mighty flat stone
                For Gwei, your Gwei
                To deposit the horror of the night
                You Majesty, our ears are wide open.

Majesty: *(The Fon is remarkably alert, articulate, without drooling, chewing or sleeping)* Thank you, Bamkov!
                Many times, I thank you.
                Today is not an ordinary day.
                Today is the day we caught our tooth!

It is the day we saw Nyuymbom at His best
Handing us two trophies in one hand
And lifting us onto His lap.
How else can we explain this?
In just one night,
The messenger of death is gone
And the evil of fear is destroyed.
Not by a troupe but by one hand
By our Gwei who is still alive;
Alive after looking death in the eyes
And thrusting his spear right into its heart.
I am yet to see one man face something this massive.
I am yet to see a man face death in the slumber of night and win.
Today, we are rewarding Gwei!
He is living proof that Bamkov will never shrink in the face of danger.
He is proof that Bamkov has taken its future into its hands.
Gwei is the tiger that lives in all of you, Bamkov.
For many years I have not given out a red feather.
What is the use of a red feather in a land mangled by death?
But today is the day our red feather regained its meaning.
Mothers and fathers of this land, our forebears are peaceful this day.
They are peaceful because the river has regained course.
They are peaceful because you finally pronounced their name correctly!
All this because a man of valor called Gwei bit the spear for us.[33]
So this is a true day for our kingdom to feast:

But in feasting, we mush humble ourselves;
We must pour our poor drink to the yawning earth.
We must hand over food to the unknown passerby,
For then the Mighty Builder will eat and belch freshness onto our land!
Bring Gwei forward for his honor.
Tawong, bring the bag of the land with the cap and red feather.

(Gwei is brought in dressed in fresh leaves over a bare chest and wearing only a wrapper thrust around and below the groin. As soon as Tawong and Yewong bring him in, shouting and ululation ensue in Chong ranks. He is placed in front of the Fon. Tawong is holding a woven tray full of beads, caps and assortments. The Fon first picks up the beads from the woven tray and puts them over Gwei's head and around his neck. After he is done, he picks up the cap, wears it on Gwei's head and inserts a red feather into the cap. Ululation come across from the female ranks as Ngwa vigilantes walk in and carry Gwei shoulder high. Manjong music occupies the whole arena as the Fon exits and Tamfu follows. As Manjong music and dancing peak, the women's ranks break as Lantir starts tearing in. Her voice is drowned by the excited women who to her surprise and shock carry her shoulder high, praise and hug her; then they sit her down in the middle of the semi circle. They dance around her and Yewong motions two young women who then approach her with a woven tray containing a cap and beads. Yewong throws beads over her shoulders, puts a cap over her head and motions the singing to stop. Yewong pronounces)

Yewong: Legend will hold that on this day, we found a Yesum:
A mother and organizer of food for the King and this kingdom!
Could any other woman have remained calm when the earth shook?

How many could celebrate cold covers in a
dry-season night?
Yesum Lantir did, because she understood the
duty Gwei had.
She knew that although Bamkov sent Gwei,
She too had to send him.
Calming his heart is the one thing he needed
most.
And what he has done shows that she did the
right thing.
His Majesty therefore requires that in honor
to our land,
In honor to those who arc their backs to feed
this land,
This cap fit into her head as a symbol of
fertility and duty:
The type that has allowed our Kingdom a
chance to survive.
Let Manjong and Chong dance as best they
can
Because today we got rid of the leopard.
This is truly the day Bamkov came back from
the dead:
The day darkness turned into day!

*(Manjong and Chong continue in a mix of integrated dancing as both
Gwei and Yesum are paraded inside the dance. As the dance reaches a
crescendo, Tamfu scampers in crying uncontrollably like a baby. Gwei
dives and grabs him first. Dancing stops abruptly and everyone rushes to
him.)*

Gwei: What is the matter Tamfu?
               Tell us quickly?

Tamfu: The F…oh God!

Gwei: The What?

Tamfu:	The F-o- oh Almighty at His Rock!
Gwei:	Hurry Up Tamfu! Hurry Up!
Tamfu:	The Fo..! Oh the Fon!
Gwei:	What has the Fon done!
Tamfu:	The Fon is…
Gwei:	Is what?
Tamfu:	Oh darkness!
Gwei:	What?
Tamfu:	Sunset!
Gwei:	Are you drunk?
Tamfu:	Sunset in Bamkov! Sunset, Gwei!
Gwei:	Sun what?
Tamfu:	Sunset over the Kingdom!

(Gwei dashes out immediately and two Nwerong masquerades appear dispersing the confused crowd. But wailing and disorder continue nonstop as people throw themselves on the ground and roll in various directions. Complete pandemonium and then darkness.
Dim light comes on slowly on Gwei, Tawong, Yewong, Yesum, Tamfu and Tangwa standing barefoot, and without caps. Yewong is carrying the bag of the Kingdom and Tawong the staff. Yesum carries a peace plant (Kikeng). Both women stoop, and are dressed in royal wrappers tied over the bosom and flowing all the way down to the feet. Two Nwerong masquerades accompany them. They stand in a semi-circle):

Tawong: *(Deliberate, and gradual)*
Bamkov! Oh Bamkov!
Kingdom of The Rock!
Who wanted to change your name?
The leopard that bled you dry sat drooling in
your palace!
The eagle that devoured its own chicks
moaned their death.
How could a lion eat its cobs seeing the
helplessness in their eyes?
Why did Nyuymbom give us a staff that
transforms into a python at night?
How could we understand all this?
Yet we have what we have,
And what we have is this land and the truth
we founded it on.
When all else fails, Nyuymbom does not.
It does not matter how long it takes,
The Mighty Builder will have his turn.
And when that time comes, this earth opens
its jaws
And swallow the taker of its children.

Gwei blow the palace horn
Let the people know that the leopard that
mauled Bamkov
Was the lion that sat on its throne.
Let them know that on his return to the
palace,
The Fon fell off his horse, groaned like a
leopard,
And burst his bulging stomach like a bubble.
His entrails littered the pathway
Like those of the leopard everyone came to
see today.
All the wounds Gwei inflicted on the leopard
Appeared on his Majesty when he fell.

He gave a yelping groan, loud like a
thunderbolt
And closed his eyes as a torrent of blood
broke from his mouth.
We came here to see the beast,
And have seen him in all Majesty;
His Majesty the beast, his Majesty the leopard!
In the name of the Mighty Builder who still
resides at His Rock,
This is indeed a happy day for the land.
The leopard will rot in the wild like a broken
pumpkin
And on its head shall grow the truth that our
Kingdom was founded on.
Send for Ngarum to take his place by The
Rock and among his people.
Gwei and Tangwa, take the lead.
We shall follow!

(Gwei blows the palace horn three times, then jumps, darts and as he opens his mouth to start the announcement, lights fade on him; sound of horn continues to fade away)

#END#

NOTES

[1] Remain Ngarum: He is known for being bitterly truthful.

[2] Rock: Short, for Rock of God, the sacred shrine of the kingdom of Bamkov, believed to be the abode of their creator and most powerful God called God-the-Builder (Nyuymbom)

[3] Kiyung-Ndzen: Also known as Kitupirr or Kutupit. This is the first village in Bamoun Kingdom after the Nso village of Ber. It was used as exile territory for Nso people who committed abominations in the Kingdom. However, it no more serves that purpose today. It is mostly populated by Nso people.

[4] Akuman: Member of a nomadic tribe who profess to cure every illness and have access to spiritual and physical layers of truth. Many of them were believed in Nso to be simply quacks.

[5] Leopard skin: Literally, on the royal bed. Legend holds that the rug surrounding the royal bed is the 'hide' of a leopard.

[6] Mairin and Mbim: Two renowned rivers in ancient Nso

[7] Disappears: Nso culture refers to their King as the Sun And to the death of a Fon as a disappearance When a Fon dies, he is said to have disappeared or that the 'sun has set'

[8] Refused to talk: Refused to summon all its forces to address the matter. Nwerong talking refers to sudden playing of Nwerong music at the instance of a crucial problem that needs to be addressed urgently.

[9] Ngong dog: Timid thieving dog

[10] Ngwa':   A hunting team for young boys. It served as a training ground for a military life in Manjong. It is used in this context to hunt down the leopard that has taken the land hostage by mauling down cattle and children. It is serving a larger vigilante role.

[11] Nyuymbom: Means 'God the Creator' in Lamnso

[12] Shinkan: Sacred wood which is generally scrubbed by chief priests and lineage heads during ritual incantations to request protection from spiritual forces.

[13] Taah: Honorific expression meaning, respectful one, elderly one, senior one, grandfather etc.

[14] Eh monja eh!   May mean something like "On the spikes `of my spear" Part of a formulaic pattern within the Ngwa' ranks that leads to the song such as the one that Tangwa intones. The song is heavily marked by

the ho-ho syllables which are possibly designed to raise emotions only. The rest of the song is repetitive and goes like this:

Introduction: *Che wu lélé, wu lélé Oh ma Bah'ah, ma Gham ahTati Njong eh dzem ah*

Chorus: *Ho-oh ho-oh!*

Intonation: **Oh suyoh vén koy yov oh**

Chorus: *Ho-oh ho –oh*

Intonation: **Suyoh**

Chorus: *Ho-oh ho-oh*

Intonation: **Oh suyoh ven koy yov oh**

Chorus: *Ho-oh ho-oh*

Intonation: **Suyoh**

Chorus: *Ho-oh ho-ho*

15 Kpéh: A hunting expression which spontaneously announces a shot with a spear. When used, it means the individual making the sound has, at the instance of the sound, released the spear towards the animal target.

16 TAV-NGWA: Literally, 'Head (Master) of Ngwa' the hunting team; therefore he should know the difference.

17 Baah   Honorific expression meaning, father.

18 Mfuh' bag   These are bags containing 'first aid' medication during war or similar exercise

¹⁹ Ntangrin — Last day on the Nso weekly calendar; also Kifeh Market day.

²⁰ Open my market: Locals believe that the first person to buy your product in the market (open the market) determines how lucky or unlucky the seller might be on that day with customers who'll make the purchases. So a market day could be "good" or "bad" depending on whether the first customer brought good luck or ill luck.

²² Nkáng: Corn beer. A local brew made out of fermented corn. One way of making it is that fermented corn is ground and mixed in water in a large container; the juice is squeezed out of the mixture and heated at very high temperatures. This boiled output is filtered and stored in calabash containers to gather more alcoholic strength for later consumption. It could be very sweet when drunk a few hours after processing or very alcoholic if it stays for days.

²³ Palm wine... head: These are symbolic elements of a Nso traditional marriage bride price ceremony. Palm wine, salt, kola nuts, etc were/are required when the bride's family accepts the groom's hand. By local law and custom, only the appropriate person with rights of betrothal over the daughter can

receive the palm wine and other
requirements of the marriage. Lineage
heads were/are also known to target
prosperous or friendly families to whom
they could give their daughters in
marriage, since marriage was/is
considered a union of families and not
just of two individuals.

24 Darkness …at noon: Will face great difficulty at an unlikely
moment; dead-end; serious misfortune.

25 Mbohlah   Means land of the dead, or spirit world,
heaven.

26 Carry palm wine: Refers to paying the bride price.
Obviously Gwei is not the right person to
receive Kibong's pride price.

27 Mother trickster: Like mother of tricks, she first
admonishes them for behaving like
children, but as soon as calm is
settling in, she starts prodding them
about the events in the morning that
led to such anger. Doing so, she does not
seem disturbed that they might get into
each other's throat again.

28 Ignite…with… leaves: Common practice within the
northwestern community in Cameroon to
use dry leaves as fuel to make a fire.

²⁹ Tav-ngwa: Literally, leader (master) of Ngwa' the
                                 hunting team.

³⁰ Tan: A hill on the south-eastern end of Nso
                                 kingdom, below which is the Ber
                                 plains.The river named Kiléiy Báh
                                 ("Leopard Watch") marks the end of Tan
                                 hill along the Ber-Jakiri road.

³¹ Chasing your shadow: Refers to the fact that Lantir is
                                 behaving like someone who is losing her
                                 mind.

³² Gwei Fon: Refers to the fact that he is now closer to
                                 the king than before and could advise the
                                 crown   on some important issues.

³³ Bite the spear :   Decided to risk his life